Quick Gluten Free Meals:

Dinner Ready in 20 Minutes or Less

Annie DePasquale, MD

FREE BONUS

As a small token of appreciation for purchasing this book, Dr. Annie would like to offer you a free copy of her next health-related e-book.

You can get your free gift by clicking here:
http://www.FamilyDocAnnie.com/glutenfree

Disclaimer

The information in this book is for informational purposes only, and is not intended to serve as a substitute for the medical treatment of a qualified physician or healthcare provider.

Acknowledgements

This book is dedicated to people thriving with Celiac disease and gluten-sensitivities. You bear a cross that most people cannot comprehend. You are an inspiration.

Introduction

Hi, I'm Annie DePasquale, a family medicine physician in Washington, D.C., who is extremely passionate about helping my patients who have dietary sensitivities.

My son was born with a multitude of food allergies and sensitivities, so I know first-hand the difficulties of finding enjoyable desserts that fit particular dietary restrictions.

For those of you with sensitivities to gluten, I hope that you thoroughly enjoy the recipes in this book.

Sincerely,
Dr. Annie

TABLE OF CONTENTS

Green Chili Chicken Tostadas with Zucchini & Tomatoes

This healthy, gluten free take on a classic Mexican comfort food will keep you warm and leave you satisfied.

Servings: 2
Prep Time: 5 minutes
Cook Time: 15 minutes

Ingredients
- 2 Tbsp olive oil, divided
- ¾ lb ground chicken
- ¼ cup onions, diced
- 1 tsp garlic, minced
- 2 cups zucchini, diced
- 1 ½ cups tomatoes, diced
- ½ cup Green Chili Enchilada Sauce
- 4 6" corn tortillas
- 2 oz feta cheese, crumbled
- ¼ cup cilantro, chopped

Directions
1. Preheat oven to 400F
2. In a pan, heat 1 Tbsp olive oil over med-high
3. Add onions & zucchini then cook 2-3 minutes
4. Add garlic & sauté 30 seconds, until fragrant
5. Add chicken & cook 6-8 minutes, breaking up with a wooden spoon as you cook
6. Rub tortillas with remaining olive oil, place on a baking sheet & bake 6-8 minutes, until crisp
7. To chicken, add tomatoes & enchilada sauce then cook 3-4 minutes to warm
8. Place tortillas on plate & top with chicken mixture then garnish with cilantro & crumbled feta

Nutrition Total
Calories: 1194 calories
Total Fat: 72 g
Cholesterol: 343 mg
Sodium: 2174 mg
Carbohydrates: 65 g
Protein: 78 g
Fiber: 13 g

Orange Chicken with Broccoli & Quinoa

Satisfy your take-out cravings in the comfort of your kitchen with this easy and delicious meal.

Servings: 2
Prep Time: 5 minutes
Cook Time: 15 minutes

Ingredients
- 2 Tbsp olive oil, divided
- 2 boneless, skinless chicken thighs, diced
- ¼ cup tapioca flour, divided
- 3 Tbsp orange marmalade
- ¼ cup orange juice
- 3 Tbsp tamari
- 1 Tbsp rice vinegar
- 1 tsp garlic, minced
- 1 Tbsp ginger, minced
- 2 cups broccoli florets
- ¼ cup low sodium chicken broth
- ¾ cup quinoa

Directions
1. In a bowl, toss chicken with half of tapioca flour, salt & pepper to coat
2. In a pot, bring 1 ½ cups water to a boil for the quinoa
3. In a pan, heat 1 Tbsp olive oil over med-high
4. Add chicken & cook 2-3 min per side, to brown
5. In a bowl, vigorously whisk marmalade, orange juice, tamari, rice vinegar, garlic, ginger & broth
6. Add remaining tapioca flour & whisk until dissolved
7. Add quinoa to boiling water, return to a boil, reduce heat, cover & simmer 12-15 minutes, until tender
8. Remove chicken from pan & set aside
9. In the same pan, heat remaining oil
10. Add broccoli florets & cook 3-4 minutes
11. Add sauce & chicken to pan & cook 6-8 minutes, until sauce is thickened & chicken is cooked through
12. Scoop quinoa into bowl then top with chicken, broccoli & sauce

Nutrition Total
Calories: 1340 calories
Total Fat: 45 g
Cholesterol: 184 mg
Sodium: 3277 mg
Carbohydrates: 170 g
Protein: 70 g
Fiber: 14 g

Blackened Honey Baked Salmon over Garlic Kale

A sweet honey glaze mixed with savory blackening seasoning will make this salmon a new favorite recipe.

Servings: 2
Prep Time: 5 minutes
Cook Time: 15 minutes

Ingredients
- 1 Tbsp olive oil
- 2 4 oz salmon fillets
- 2 tsp honey
- 1 Tbsp blackening seasoning
- 1 tsp garlic, minced
- 3 cups kale, chopped
- 1 lemon, juiced & zested

Directions
1. Preheat oven to 375F
2. Line a baking sheet with parchment paper
3. Rub salmon filets with honey then sprinkle liberally with blackening seasoning, salt & pepper
4. Place on prepared baking sheet & roast 15-18 minutes, until cooked through
5. In a pan, heat olive oil over med
6. Add garlic & cook 30 seconds, until fragrant
7. Add lemon juice & kale then sauté 5-7 minutes, until kale is tender
8. Remove kale from heat & toss with lemon zest
9. Enjoy salmon with kale on the side

Nutrition Total
Calories: 547 calories
Total Fat: 31 g
Cholesterol: 145 mg
Sodium: 2196 mg
Carbohydrates: 20 g
Protein: 52 g
Fiber: 2 g

Fish Tacos with Chili Lime Slaw

You'll love the zesty flavors and easy preparation of these savory fish tacos.

Servings: 2
Prep Time: 10 minutes
Cook Time: 10 minutes

Ingredients
- 8 oz flounder fillets
- ¼ cup brown rice flour
- 1 Tbsp paprika
- 1 Tbsp olive oil
- 2 cups cabbage, shredded
- ½ cup carrots, shredded
- 2 Tbsp Greek yogurt
- ¼ cup cilantro
- 1 lime, juiced
- 1 tsp chili powder
- 4 corn tortillas

Directions
1. Pat fish fillets dry
2. In a re-sealable bag, combine rice flour, paprika salt & pepper then add fish fillets & toss to coat
3. Heat olive oil over medium heat
4. Add fish & cook 3-5 minutes per side, until cooked through
5. In a bowl, whisk together Greek yogurt, cilantro, lime juice, ground chipotle, salt & pepper
6. Add cabbage & carrots & toss to coat
7. Warm tortillas
8. Place fish fillet into tortilla & top with slaw

Nutrition Total
Calories: 781 calories
Total Fat: 27 g
Cholesterol: 111 mg
Sodium: 906 mg
Carbohydrates: 101 g
Protein: 42 g
Fiber: 17 g

Buffalo Cauliflower Sandwiches with Spice Roasted Sweet Potatoes

This vegetable-centered take on a classic buffalo sandwiches is easy and full of flavor.

Servings: 2
Prep Time: 5 minutes
Cook Time: 15 minutes

Ingredients
- 1 ½ cups cauliflower, chopped
- ¼ cup brown rice flour
- 2 Tbsp olive oil, divided
- 2 gluten free buns
- 3 Tbsp salted butter
- 3 Tbsp hot sauce
- 2 Tbsp pickles, sliced
- 1 ½ cups sweet potatoes, diced
- 1 tsp paprika
- 1 tsp cumin

Directions
1. Preheat oven to 400F
2. In a pan, heat 1 Tbsp olive oil
3. Add cauliflower, salt & pepper then cook 8-10 minutes, until tender
4. On a sheet pan, toss sweet potatoes with remaining olive oil, paprika, cumin, salt & pepper then roast 15-20 minutes, until tender
5. Remove cauliflower to a bowl & toss with brown rice flour
6. In pan used for cauliflower, melt butter then add hot sauce & whisk to combine
7. Add cauliflower to buffalo sauce & toss to coat
8. Warm buns in oven 2-3 minutes
9. Scoop buffalo cauliflower onto buns and top with pickles. Enjoy sweet potatoes on the side.

Nutrition Total
Calories: 1457 calories
Total Fat: 74 g
Cholesterol: 92 mg
Sodium: 2529 mg
Carbohydrates: 189 g
Protein: 18 g
Fiber: 25 g

Turkey Chili with Sweet Potatoes & Chickpeas

Get slow cooker flavors in just 20 minutes with this easy and healthy turkey chili.

Servings: 2
Prep Time: 5 minutes
Cook Time: 15 minutes

Ingredients
- 1 Tbsp olive oil
- ½ cup onion, diced
- ½ cup red bell pepper, diced
- 1 cup sweet potatoes, small diced
- ¾ lb extra lean ground turkey
- 1 Tbsp chili
- 1 Tbsp smoked paprika
- ½ Tbsp cumin
- ½ tsp oregano
- 1 cup chickpeas
- 1 ½ cup tomatoes, diced
- 1 Tbsp balsamic vinegar
- 1 cup chicken broth
- ¼ cup Mexican cheese, shredded
- 2 Tbsp sour cream
- 2 Tbsp chives

Directions
1. In a pan, heat olive oil
2. Add onions, bell peppers & sweet potatoes then cook 3-5 minutes
3. Add turkey, chili powder, smoked paprika, cumin & oregano then cook 5-8 min, breaking up with a wooden spoon as you cook
4. Add chickpeas, tomatoes, balsamic vinegar & chicken broth and bring to a boil then reduce heat to medium-low & simmer 10-12 minutes
5. Scoop chili into bowls then garnish with shredded cheese, sour cream & chives

Nutrition Total
Calories: 1448 calories
Total Fat: 43 g
Cholesterol: 276 mg
Sodium: 1686 mg
Carbohydrates: 134 g
Protein: 142 g
Fiber: 34 g

Mediterranean Frittata with Sun Dried Tomatoes, Spinach & Feta

Fresh flavors inspired by the Mediterranean fill this fluffy frittata.

Servings: 2
Prep Time: 5 minutes
Cook Time: 15 minutes

Ingredients
- 4 large eggs
- 1 Tbsp salted butter
- ¾ cup whole milk
- ¼ cup low sodium tomato juice
- ¼ tsp dried thyme
- ¼ tsp dried oregano
- ¼ cup sun dried tomatoes, chopped
- 1 cup spinach, chopped
- 2 oz feta, crumbled

Directions
1. In a bowl, whisk together eggs, milk, tomato juice, thyme, oregano, salt & pepper until well combined
2. Add sun dried tomatoes & spinach and stir to incorporate
3. Melt butter in a large pan over medium heat
4. Add egg mixture, sprinkle with feta, reduce heat to medium-low, cover & cook 8-10 minutes until set & cooked through
5. Remove from heat, keeping covered & let stand 5-7 minutes
6. Cut frittata into wedges & enjoy

Nutrition Total
Calories: 725 calories
Total Fat: 51 g
Cholesterol: 845 mg
Sodium: 982 mg
Carbohydrates: 24 g
Protein: 42 g
Fiber: 2.6 g

Tofu Lo Mein with Mushrooms & Zucchini Noodles

Get the comfort of this familiar noodle dish without the heavy carbs.

Servings: 2
Prep Time: 5 minutes
Cook Time: 10 minutes

Ingredients
- 1 Tbsp olive oil
- ½ lb firm tofu, cubed
- ¼ lb mushrooms, sliced
- ½ cup carrots, shredded
- 1 tsp garlic
- 2 green onions, sliced
- 2 Tbsp tamari
- 1 Tbsp gluten free hoisin sauce
- 1 tsp honey
- 1 tsp sesame oil
- 1 tsp ginger
- 2 cups zucchini, spiralized
- 2 Tbsp cilantro, chopped
- 2 Tbsp mint, chopped

Directions
1. In a pan, heat olive oil over medium
2. Add tofu & sear 2-3 min per side then remove & set aside
3. Add garlic, mushrooms, green onion, carrots & zucchini noodles then sauté 3-4 minutes, until tender
4. In a bowl, whisk together tamari, hoisin sauce, honey, sesame oil & ginger
5. Add sauce & tofu to pan & cook 2-3 minutes, stirring to coat
6. Scoop lo mein onto plate & garnish with cilantro & mint

Nutrition Total
Calories: 563 calories
Total Fat: 33 g
Cholesterol: 1 mg
Sodium: 2364 mg
Carbohydrates: 38 g
Protein: 39 g
Fiber: 8 g

Double Decker Spicy Black Bean Veggie Burgers with Lemon Aioli

You won't miss the meat with these deliciously spiced patties.

Servings: 2
Prep Time: 10 minutes
Cook Time: 10 minutes

Ingredients
- 2 Tbsp olive oil, divided
- 1 cup black beans, drained & rinsed
- ¼ cup onion, diced
- 1 egg
- 1 tsp garlic, minced
- ¼ cup cilantro, chopped
- 2 Tbsp chives, chopped
- 1/2 cup gluten free panko breadcrumbs
- 1 tsp each: chili powder, cumin, coriander, smoked paprika
- 1 lemon, juiced & zested
- 2 Tbsp Greek yogurt
- 2 Tbsp mayo
- 2 gluten free buns

Directions
1. In a pan, heat olive oil over medium-high
2. Add onion & cook 2-3 minutes, until soft
3. In a bowl, smash black beans with the back of a fork
4. Add onion, egg, garlic, cilantro, chives, gluten free breadcrumbs, chili powder, cumin, coriander, smoked paprika, lemon zest salt & pepper and stir to combine well
5. In pan used for onions, heat remaining olive oil
6. Form black bean mixture into 4 thin patties then add patties to hot pan & cook 4-5 min per side
7. In a bowl, whisk together lemon juice, Greek yogurt & mayo
8. Warm buns if desired
9. Slather buns with aioli and layer black bean patties on top

Nutrition Total
Calories: 1354 calories
Total Fat: 67 g
Cholesterol: 207 mg
Sodium: 1912 mg
Carbohydrates: 170 g
Protein: 24 g
Fiber: 20 g

Blackened Steak Salad with Apples, Wilted Spinach & Goat Cheese

Enjoy the umami flavors of thinly sliced steak with a sweet balsamic dressing in this easy, savory salad.

Servings: 2
Prep Time: 5 minutes
Cook Time: 10 minutes

Ingredients
- ¼ cup olive oil, divided
- ½ lb flank steak, trimmed
- 1 apple, cored & thinly sliced
- 4 cups spinach
- ¼ cup red onions, thinly sliced
- 4 oz goat cheese, crumbled
- 2 Tbsp white balsamic
- 1 tsp Dijon mustard

Directions
1. In a pan, heat 1 Tbsp olive oil over medium-high
2. Add steak & sear 3-7 minutes per side, or to desired doneness, then allow to rest for 5 minutes
3. In a bowl, vigorously whisk together balsamic, remaining olive oil & Dijon mustard until emulsified
4. In a separate pan, heat 1 Tbsp olive oil
5. Add red onions & cook 1-2 min then remove from heat & add spinach & ½ of dressing & toss to wilt
6. Thinly slice steak
7. Scoop spinach onto plate, top with sliced apples, crumbled goat cheese & sliced steak then drizzle with remaining dressing

Nutrition Total
Calories: 1357 calories
Total Fat: 102 g
Cholesterol: 209 mg
Sodium: 1055 mg
Carbohydrates: 39 g
Protein: 75 g
Fiber: 8 g

Spaghetti Carbonara with Spinach, Pancetta & Parmesan

Indulge in the creamy goodness of a classic carbonara over gluten free noodles.

Servings: 2
Prep Time: 10 minutes
Cook Time: 10 minutes

Ingredients
- 6 oz gluten free spaghetti
- 1 large eggs
- 2 Tbsp parmesan, grated
- 1 /2 Tbsp olive oil, divided
- 3 oz pancetta, diced
- 2 cups spinach, roughly chopped
- 2 tsp garlic
- 1 Tbsp parsley, chopped

Directions
1. Bring a large pot of water to a boil & cook pasta according to directions on package then drain, reserving about ¼ cup pasta water for sauce
2. In a bowl, lightly whisk eggs & parmesan
3. In a pan, heat olive oil over medium-high heat then add pancetta & cook 5-7 minutes, until just crisp
4. Add garlic & cook 30 seconds, until fragrant
5. Add spinach & stir 1-2 minutes to wilt
6. Remove from heat, add pasta & egg mixture & quickly toss to combine
7. Add reserved pasta water 2 Tbsp at a time until creamy consistency is reached
8. Scoop pasta into bowls & garnish with parsley

Nutrition Total
Calories: 722 calories
Total Fat: 31 g
Cholesterol: 197 mg
Sodium: 1916 mg
Carbohydrates: 72 g
Protein: 37 g
Fiber: 4 g

Cumin Curry Lamb Meatballs with Herbed Cauliflower Rice

Spice things up with these easy cumin curry meatballs made with sweet ground lamb and served over herbaceous cauliflower rice.

Servings: 2
Prep Time: 10 minutes
Cook Time: 10 minutes

Ingredients
- 8 oz ground lamb
- 1 egg
- 2 Tbsp curry
- 1 Tbsp cumin
- ¼ cup onion, minced
- 1 tsp garlic, minced
- 3 Tbsp olive oil, divided
- 1 ½ cups cauliflower rice
- 1 lemon, juiced & zested
- 1 Tbsp tarragon, chopped
- 1 Tbsp cilantro, chopped

Directions
1. In a bowl, combine lamb, egg, curry, cumin, onion, garlic, salt & pepper then form into 6-8 meatballs
2. In a pan, heat 2 Tbsp olive oil over medium-high heat
3. Add meatballs & cook 3-5 min per side, until cooked through
4. In a separate pan, heat remaining olive oil then add cauliflower rice
5. Add cauliflower rice & cook 5-7 minutes, until tender
6. Remove cauliflower rice from heat then add lemon juice, lemon zest & herbs
7. Scoop cauliflower rice onto plate & top with meatballs

Nutrition Total
Calories: 1223 calories
Total Fat: 102 g
Cholesterol: 352 mg
Sodium: 636 mg
Carbohydrates: 25 g
Protein: 52 g
Fiber: 12 g

Chimichurri Tofu over Cold Basmati Rice & Cucumber Salad

Packed with fresh herbs and veggies, this is an easy dish that will leave you feeling great.

Servings: 2
Prep Time: 10 minutes
Cook Time: 10 minutes

Ingredients
- ½ lb tofu, sliced
- 2 cloves garlic
- 2 Tbsp parsley
- 2 Tbsp cilantro
- 1 Tbsp oregano
- ¼ cup olive oil, divided
- 1 lime, juiced
- ¾ cup basmati rice
- 1 cup cucumbers, diced

Directions
1. Bring 1 ½ cup salted water to a boil for the rice
2. In a food processor or high-speed blender, pulse garlic, parsley, cilantro, oregano, 3 Tbsp olive oil, lime juice, salt & pepper until blended but still chunky
3. Pour chimichurri sauce into a bowl and add tofu then toss to coat & allow to marinate 3-5 minutes
4. Add rice to boiling water & cook 12-15 minutes, until tender
5. In a pan, heat remaining olive oil over medium-high
6. Remove tofu from marinade (reserve marinade) & add to hot pan then cook 3-5 minute per side
7. Place rice in strainer and run under cool water
8. In a bowl, combine cucumbers, rice & remaining marinade
9. Scoop rice into bowl & top with tofu

Nutrition Total
Calories: 1295 calories
Total Fat: 67 g
Cholesterol: 0 mg
Sodium: 44 mg
Carbohydrates: 137 g
Protein: 41 g
Fiber: 5 g

Honey Lime Ginger Pork Chops with Sautéed Arugula & Peppers

Savory pork chops get a sweet glaze and a heaping side of veggies.

Servings: 2
Prep Time: 5 minutes
Cook Time: 15 minutes

Ingredients
- 8 oz boneless pork chops
- 1 tsp honey
- 1 Tbsp tamari
- 1 Tbsp ginger, minced
- 1 lime, juiced
- 2 Tbsp olive oil, divided
- ¼ cup red onions, sliced
- 1 cup bell peppers, diced
- 2 cups arugula, chopped

Directions
1. In a pan, heat 1 Tbsp olive oil over med-high
2. Pat pork chops dry, sprinkle with salt & pepper then add to hot pan & cook 4-7 minutes per side, until just cooked through
3. In a separate pan, heat remaining olive oil over medium heat
4. Add onions & bell peppers cook 3-4 minutes, until soft
5. Add arugula, salt & pepper then stir to wilt
6. In a bowl, whisk together honey, tamari, ginger & lime juice
7. When pork chops are just cooked through, add honey lime ginger sauce to pan & cook an additional 1-2 minutes, until slightly thickened
8. Place pork chops on plate & top with remaining sauce. Enjoy arugula & peppers on the side

Nutrition Total
Calories: 662 calories
Total Fat: 36 g
Cholesterol: 150 mg
Sodium: 1140 mg
Carbohydrates: 29 g
Protein: 56 g
Fiber: 5 g

Coffee Rubbed Pork Chops with Sweet Potato Mash

Coffee compliments these savory pork chops perfectly, on a sweet bed of sweet potato mash.

Servings: 2
Prep Time: 5 minutes
Cook Time: 15 minutes

Ingredients
- 8 oz boneless pork chops
- 1 Tbsp coffee beans, finely ground
- 1 tsp honey
- 1 tsp brown sugar
- 1 tsp paprika
- 2 Tbsp olive oil, divided
- 1 ½ cups sweet potatoes, small diced
- ½ cup unsweetened almond milk
- 1 Tbsp unsalted butter

Directions
1. Preheat over to 400F
2. Place sweet potatoes in a pot, cover with water, bring to a boil over high heat then reduce, cover & cook 10-12 minutes, until tender
3. In a bowl, whisk together coffee, honey, brown sugar, paprika, 1 Tbsp olive oil, salt & pepper then rub on both sides of pork chops
4. In a pan, heat remaining olive oil then add pork chops & cook 4-7 minutes per side, until cooked through
5. When sweet potatoes are tender, drain return to pan, add milk & butter then mash
6. Scoop sweet potato mash onto plate & top with coffee rubbed pork chops

Nutrition Total
Calories: 1081 calories
Total Fat: 50 g
Cholesterol: 180 mg
Sodium: 422 mg
Carbohydrates: 102 g
Protein: 61 g
Fiber: 19 g

ABOUT THE AUTHOR

Annie DePasquale MD is an actively practicing family physician and mother of two - soon-to-be three! When not caring for her family or patients, she is helping to spread good family medicine practices through her writing and social media pursuits.

Visit her at **http://www.FamilyDocAnnie.com**

She is also on Facebook and Twitter. #FamilyDocAnnie

If you enjoyed this book, please leave a quick review on Amazon. This would be tremendously appreciated.

OTHER BOOKS

Dr. Annie DePasquale's other published books include:

Gluten Free Desserts: 30 Delicious Recipes

Delectable Diabetes Desserts: 30 Recipes With 10 Carbs or Less

Diabetes & Hypertension Cookbook: 45 Recipes for Low Carb / Low Salt Diet

Cooking With Kids: 30 Healthy Recipes Your Kids Will Love To Make

Stop Smoking Now

Stress Less: 50 Practical Tips to Decrease Your Daily Stress

FREE BONUS

As a small token of appreciation for purchasing this book, Dr. Annie would like to offer you a free copy of her next health-related e-book.

You can get your free gift by clicking here:
http://www.FamilyDocAnnie.com/glutenfree

Printed in Great Britain
by Amazon